T. Nessman

1·2·3 PUPPETS

Written by Jean Warren

Illustrated by Cora L. Walker

Simple Puppets To Make For Working With Young Children

Warren Publishing House, Inc.
Everett, Washington

Editor: Gayle Bittinger
Contributing Editor: Elizabeth S. McKinnon
Assistant Editor: Claudia G. Reid
Layout and Cover Design: Kathy Jones
Cover Illustration: Marion Hopping Ekberg

ISBN 0-911019-21-9

Library of Congress Catalog Number 89-050122
Printed in the United States of America
Published by: Warren Publishing House, Inc.
        P.O. Box 2250
        Everett, WA 98203

Introduction

Puppets are a unique teaching tool. They can be used to teach concepts, to expand language and listening skills and to encourage creative thinking. Puppets are great for using at transition times, circle times and music times.

1•2•3 PUPPETS is a collection of simple puppets to make for working with young children. Each puppet is presented as a specific character and is accompanied by a song or a poem. Several of the puppets also have patterns to use as guides when making them. However, the best thing about these puppets is their versatility. As shown in the many illustrated variations, each puppet is capable of becoming any number of characters. We encourage you to adapt the puppets to meet your individual needs.

Note: The puppets suggested in this book are intended for use by parents and teachers. If you decide to have young children make or play with the puppets, avoid using materials that could be accidentally swallowed.

Contents

Puppets

Family Tube ———————————— 8
Nursery Rhyme ———————————— 9
Happy Face/Sad Face Paper Plate ———————— 10
Circle Shape ———————————— 11
Polka Dot ———————————— 12
Teddy Bear ———————————— 13
Circus Shadow ———————————— 14
Clothespin Clown ———————————— 15
Owl Paper Plate ———————————— 16
Paper Spider ———————————— 17
Tissue Ghost ———————————— 18
Jack-O'-Lantern Mask ———————————— 19
Talking Turkey Paper ———————————— 20
Turkey Hand ———————————— 21
Hanukkah Candle ———————————— 22
Peek-A-Boo Elf ———————————— 23
Reindeer Triangle ———————————— 24
Santa Felt Triangle ———————————— 25
Snow Pal Felt Hand ———————————— 26
Groundhog Pop-Up ———————————— 27
Queen of Hearts Paper Bag ———————— 28
Abe Lincoln Tongue Depressor ———————— 29
Clothespin Pancake Man ———————————— 30
Lion and Lamb Paper Plate ———————— 31
Leprechaun Styrofoam Ball ———————— 32
Caterpillar String ———————————— 33
Butterfly Straw ———————————— 34
Willie Worm Surprise ———————————— 35
Pom-Pom Chick ———————————— 36
Walking Duck ———————————— 37
Egg Carton Pig ———————————— 38
Buzzy Bee Balloon ———————————— 39
Little Dog Cup ———————————— 40
Frog Paper Plate ———————————— 41

Contents

Puppets *(Continued)*

Fish Envelope _____ 42
Turtle Bowl _____ 43
Alligator Egg Carton _____ 44
Dinosaur Sock _____ 45
Sun Circle _____ 46
Hula Dancer Whisk Broom _____ 47
Robot Box _____ 48
Popsicle Stick Car _____ 49
Nosy Rosie Cup _____ 50
Bertha Bottle _____ 51
Lemon and Lime Rhythm _____ 52
Dish Mop _____ 53
Hairbrush _____ 54
MacBurger _____ 55
French Fry Holder Marching Band _____ 56
Millie Milk Carton _____ 57
Dancing Spoon _____ 58
Goldilocks Folded Paper _____ 59
Fingertip Friend _____ 60
Finger Face Family _____ 61
Paper Plate Finger Puppet Theater _____ 62

Puppet Patterns

Nursery Rhyme _____ 64
Circus Shadow _____ 66
Jack-O'-Lantern Mask _____ 68
Santa Felt Triangle _____ 69
Snow Pal Felt Hand _____ 70
Lion and Lamb Paper Plate _____ 72
Butterfly Straw _____ 74
Walking Duck _____ 75
Turtle Bowl _____ 76
Paper Plate Finger Puppet Theater _____ 77

Puppets

Family Tube Puppets

My Family
Sung to: "The Mulberry Bush"

Oh, come and meet my family,
My family, my family.
Oh, come and meet my family,
They live at home with me.

Jean Warren

Materials: Cardboard toilet tissue tubes; felt scraps; plastic moving eyes; construction paper; yarn; Popsicle sticks; glue; pair of scissors.

Making the Puppets: Cut cardboard toilet tissue tubes into a variety of sizes. Decorate each tube to look like a different family member: a mother, a father, a brother, a sister, a baby, a grandmother and a grandfather. Use felt scraps and construction paper to make nose, mouth, and clothing shapes and glue them to the tubes. Add two plastic moving eyes to each puppet. Glue on pieces of yarn for hair or cut slits in the tops of the tubes and curl them. Glue Popsicle sticks inside the bottoms of the tubes for handles.

Variations:

Nursery Rhyme Finger Puppets

Let's All Sing Some Nursery Rhymes
Sung to: "Mary Had a Little Lamb"

Let's all sing some nursery rhymes,
Nursery rhymes, nursery rhymes.
Let's all sing some nursery rhymes
With our puppets today.

Let's sing about the little lamb,
Little lamb, little lamb.
Let's sing about the little lamb
Who went to school one day.

Let's sing about Jack and Jill,
Jack and Jill, Jack and Jill.
Let's sing about Jack and Jill
Who climbed right up the hill.

Let's sing about Little Bo Peep,
Little Bo Peep, Little Bo Peep.
Let's sing about Little Bo Peep
Who lost all her sheep.

Jean Warren

Materials: Clear self-stick paper; felt-tip markers; tape; pair of scissors.

Making the Puppets: Photocopy the puppet patterns on pages 64 and 65. Use felt-tip markers to color the patterns. Cover both sides of the patterns with clear self-stick paper and cut them out. Bend the tabs behind the puppets and fasten them with tape.

Variations:

Happy Face/Sad Face Paper Plate Puppet

I'm a Smiley, Happy Face
Sung to: "I'm a Little Teapot"

I'm a smiley, happy face,
Watch me grin.
Great big smile
From my forehead to my chin.
When I am upset and things are bad,
Then my happy face turns to sad.

Jean Warren

Materials: Paper plates; felt-tip markers; tongue depressor; yarn; stapler; glue; pair of scissors.

Making the Puppet: Glue a tongue depressor handle to the front of a paper plate. Place another paper plate over the first one, fronts facing, and staple the plates together. Glue pieces of yarn for hair on top of both plates so that it hangs down on both sides. Then use felt-tip markers to decorate one side of the puppet with a happy face and the other side with a sad face.

Variations:

Circle Shape Puppet

Circle Puppet, Circle Puppet

Circle Puppet, Circle Puppet, jump up high,
Circle Puppet, Circle Puppet, fly, fly, fly.

Circle Puppet, Circle Puppet, bend down low,
Circle Puppet, Circle Puppet, there you go.

Circle Puppet, Circle Puppet, twirl around,
Circle Puppet, Circle Puppet, touch the ground.

Circle Puppet, Circle Puppet, hop, hop, hop,
Circle Puppet, Circle Puppet, now you stop.

Adapted Traditional

Materials: Construction paper; felt-tip markers; Popsicle stick; glue; pair of scissors.

Making the Puppet: Cut one large circle and four small circles out of a piece of construction paper. Then cut two 6-inch and two 4-inch strips out of construction paper. Fold the strips accordion-style. Glue the shorter pieces to the large circle for arms and the longer pieces to the circle for legs. Attach the small circles to the ends of the folded paper strips for hands and feet. Glue a Popsicle stick handle to the back of the large circle. Add facial features with felt tip markers.

Variations:

Polka Dot Puppets

Polka Dot Poem

Five (name of color) polka dots lay on the floor,
One sat up and then there were four.
Four (name of color) polka dots got on their knees,
One tipped over and then there were three.
Three (name of color) polka dots stood on one shoe,
One fell down and then there were two.
Two (name of color) polka dots started to run,
One stopped quickly and then there was one.
One (name of color) polka dot rolled toward the door,
When it disappeared there were no more.

Janet Hoffman
Elmira, NY

Materials: Self-stick circles of the same color.

Making the Puppets: Attach a self-stick circle of the same color to each finger of one hand.

Variations:

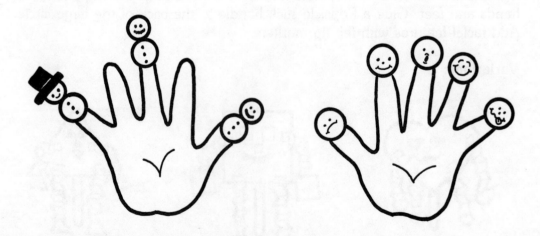

Teddy Bear Puppet

Did You Ever See a Teddy Bear?
Sung to: "Did You Ever See a Lassie?"

Did you ever see a teddy bear,
A teddy bear, a teddy bear?
Did you ever see a teddy bear
Go this way and that?
Go this way and that way,
And this way and that way.
Did you ever see a teddy bear
Go this way and that?

Mary Evelyn Barcus
Indianapolis, IN

Materials: Stuffed teddy bear; polyester stuffing (available at fabric and craft stores); pair of scissors.

Making the Puppet: Cut a slit in the back of a teddy bear and carefully remove the stuffing. Partially restuff the bear with polyester stuffing. Insert your hand in the bear's back and extend your fingers into its arms and head.

Variations:

Circus Shadow Puppets

Circus Song
Sung to: "Mary Had a Little Lamb"

Let's all go to the circus tent,
Circus tent, circus tent.
Let's all go to the circus tent
And see what we can see.

We will watch the elephants march,
Elephants march, elephants march.
We will watch the elephants march
Around the circus ring.

We will watch the dancing bears,
Dancing bears, dancing bears.
We will watch the horses prance
Around the circus ring.

We will watch the clowns play tricks,
Clowns play tricks, clowns play tricks.
We will watch the clowns play tricks
In the circus ring.

Jean Warren

Materials: Posterboard; Popsicle sticks; glue; pair of scissors.

Making the Puppets: Use the patterns on pages 66 and 67 as guides to cut circus shapes out of posterboard. Glue a Popsicle stick handle to each shape. Shine a bright light on a wall. Hold the puppets in front of the light to make shadows.

Variations:

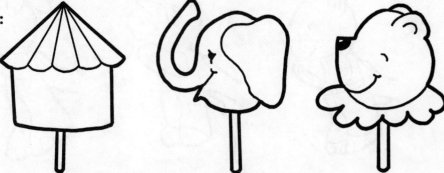

Clothespin Clown Puppet

Did You Ever See a Clown?
Sung to: "Did You Ever See a Lassie?"

Did you ever see a clown,
A clown, a clown?
Did you ever see a clown
Move this way and that?
Move this way and that way,
Move this way and that way.
Did you ever see a clown
Move this way and that?

Paula C. Foreman
Millersville, PA

Materials: Slot-type clothespin; felt scraps; felt-tip markers; glue; pair of scissors.

Making the Puppet: Use felt-tip markers to draw a clown face on the rounded knob of a slot-type clothespin and a polka-dotted costume on the sides of the clothespin. Glue on a ruffled collar and a clown hat cut out of felt scraps. To store your puppet, slip the clothespin over the rim of an empty coffee can or other container.

Variations:

Owl Paper Plate Puppet

Have You Seen the Little Gray Owl?
Sung to: "The Muffin Man"

Have you seen the little gray owl,
The little gray owl, the little gray owl?
Have you seen the little gray owl,
Who sits in the big oak tree?

He sits all night and winks at me,
Winks at me, winks at me.
He sits all night and winks at me,
The little gray owl in the tree.

Jean Warren

Materials: Paper plates; construction paper; felt-tip markers; stapler; glue; pair of scissors.

Making the Puppet: Cut a paper plate in half. Position one half over the top of a whole paper plate with the fronts of the plates facing. Staple the plates together. Use construction paper and felt-tip markers to create an owl face on the back of the whole paper plate. Put your hand in the pocket on the back of the puppet to make it move.

Variations:

 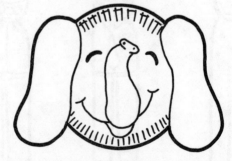 

Paper Spider Finger Puppet

Spin, Spin Little Spider
Sung to: "Ten Little Indians"

Spin, spin, little spider,
Spin, spin, wider, wider.
Spin, spin, little spider,
Early in the morning.

Dance, dance, little spider,
Dance, dance, dance out wider.
Dance, dance, little spider,
Early in the morning.

Additional verses: "Run, run, little spider;
Crawl, crawl, little spider; Jump, jump, little spider."

Jean Warren

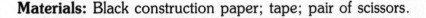

Materials: Black construction paper; tape; pair of scissors.

Making the Puppet: Cut a 2-inch square out of black construction paper.
Wrap the square snugly around the tip of a finger and tape it securely near
the top. Cut slits around the bottom of the puppet to make legs. Fold the
legs out.

Variations:

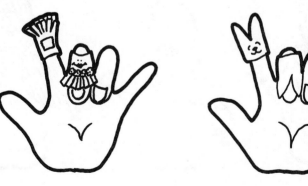

Tissue Ghost Puppet

Friendly Ghost
Sung to: "Frere Jacques"

I'm a friendly ghost, I'm a friendly ghost,
Watch me fly, watch me fly.
I can fly right through the air,
See how all the people stare.
Way up high, in the sky.

Jean Warren

Materials: White facial tissue; rubber band; black felt-tip marker.

Making the Puppet: Place a white facial tissue over the tip of one finger. Wrap a rubber band around the tissue at the first bend in the finger to form a head. Use a black felt-tip marker to add facial features to the puppet.

Variations:

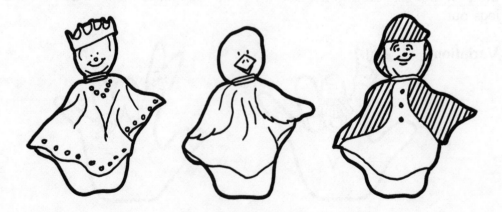

Jack-O'-Lantern Mask Puppet

I Was a Pumpkin
Sung to: "Oh, My Darling Clementine"

I was a pumpkin, a big fat pumpkin,
I was growing on a vine.
Then you carved a jack-o'-lantern,
And I turned out just fine.

Sue Brown
Louisville, KY

Materials: Orange posterboard; pencil; Popsicle stick; craft knife; glue; pair of scissors.

Making the Puppet: Use the pattern on page 68 as a guide to cut a pumpkin shape out of orange posterboard. Use a pencil to sketch a jack-o'-lantern face on the shape. Cut out the pumpkin facial features with a craft knife and glue a Popsicle stick handle to the back.

Variations:

Talking Turkey Paper Puppet

Hello, Mr. Turkey
Sung to: "If You're Happy and You Know It"

Hello, Mr. Turkey, how are you?
Hello, Mr. Turkey, how are you?
With a gobble, gobble, gobble,
And a wobble, wobble, wobble.
Hello, Mr. Turkey, how are you?

Barbara H. Jackson
Denton, TX

Materials: Brown construction paper; felt-tip markers; construction paper scraps; glue; pair of scissors.

Making the Puppet: Fold a piece of brown construction paper as shown below. Use felt-tip markers and construction paper scraps to create a turkey face on the front flap. Then cut turkey leg shapes out of brown construction paper and glue them to the bottom of the puppet.

Variations:

Turkey Hand Puppet

My Turkey

I have a turkey, big and fat.
He spreads his wings
And walks like that.
His daily corn he would not miss,
And when he talks, he sounds like this
Gobble, gobble, gobble.

Dee Hoffman, Judy Panko
Aitkin, MN

Materials: Construction paper; felt-tip markers; Popsicle stick; glue; pair of scissors.

Making the Puppet: Cut a hand shape out of construction paper. Glue a Popsicle stick handle to the bottom of the shape. Use felt-tip markers to color the fingers like feathers and to draw a turkey face on the thumb.

Variations:

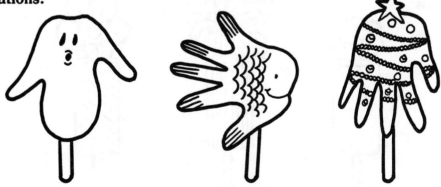

Hanukkah Candle Puppet

Lighting All the Candles
Sung to: "I've Been Working on the Railroad"

I am lighting all the candles
On this Hanukkah night.
I am lighting all the candles
To see them shining bright.
Flicker, flicker, little candles,
Fill me with your glow.
Now the times has come to count them,
Ready, set and go —
1-2-3-4-5-6-7-8.

Gillian Whitman
Westfield, NJ

Materials: Cardboard toilet tissue tube; yellow construction paper; Popsicle stick; tempera paint; paint brush; glue; pair of scissors.

Making the Puppet: Paint a cardboard toilet tissue tube with tempera paint and allow it to dry. Cut a flame shape out of yellow construction paper. Glue the shape to the top of a Popsicle stick. Slip the toilet tissue tube over the Popsicle stick and flame. "Light" the candle puppet by pushing the flame above the top of the tube.

Variations:

Peek-A-Boo Elf Puppet

Mr. Elf
Sung to: "Frere Jacques"

Mr. Elf, Mr. Elf,
Where are you? Where are you?
Are you making toys
For all the girls and boys?
Peek-a-boo! I see you!

Gayle Bittinger

Materials: 1-inch Styrofoam ball; cardboard toilet tissue tube; straw; red felt scraps; felt-tip markers; yarn; glue; pair of scissors.

Making the Puppet: Push one end of a straw into a 1-inch Styrofoam ball to make a hole. Remove the straw and fill the hole with glue. Put the end of the straw back into the hole and allow the glue to dry. Use felt-tip markers to draw eyes, a nose and a mouth on the Styrofoam ball. Glue on pieces of yarn for hair. Cut two small triangles out of red felt scraps and glue them together along two sides to make a hat. Glue the hat to the top of the Styrofoam ball. Put the straw down through a cardboard toilet tissue tube and let the Elf Puppet play peek-a-boo with the children.

Variations:

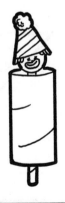

Reindeer Triangle Puppet

Did You Ever See a Reindeer?
Sung to: "Did You Ever See a Lassie?"

Did you ever see a reindeer,
A reindeer, a reindeer?
Did you ever see a reindeer
With a bright shiny nose?
A bright shiny nose,
A bright shiny nose.
Did you ever see a reindeer
With a bright shiny nose?

Cheryl Heltne
Katy, TX

Materials: Brown posterboard; twigs; black and red construction paper; Popsicle stick; tape; glue; pair of scissors.

Making the Puppet: Cut a triangle out of brown posterboard for a reindeer face. Tape two twigs to the back of the triangle for antlers. Then glue on two black construction paper circles for eyes and a red construction paper circle for a nose. Complete the puppet by attaching a Popsicle stick handle to the back.

Barb Mazzochi
Villa Park, IL

Variations:

Santa Felt Triangle Puppet

S-A-N-T-A
Sung to: "Old MacDonald Had a Farm"

Who laughs this way — "Ho-ho-ho?"
S-A-N-T-A!
Who drives the sleigh through sleet or snow?
S-A-N-T-A!
His hair is white, his suit is red,
He wears a hat to cover his head.
Who brings fun for girls and boys?
S-A-N-T-A!

Debra Lindahl
Libertyville, IL

Materials: Red felt; white pom-pom; needle and thread; cotton ball; felt scraps; glue; pair of scissors.

Making the Puppet: Use the pattern on page 69 as a guide to cut two large triangles out of red felt. Sew the triangles together along two sides, leaving a 2-inch finger hole in the middle of each side as indicated on the pattern. Glue a white pom-pom to the top of the triangle. Cut a strip out of a felt scrap for Santa's face and glue it to the front of the puppet. Add felt eye and nose shapes. Fluff out a cotton ball and glue it below the nose for a beard. Add a belt and a buckle shape cut out of felt to complete the puppet.

Variations:

Snow Pal Felt Hand Puppet

I'm a Friendly Snow Pal
Sung to: "I'm a Little Teapot"

I'm a friendly snow pal, big and fat,
Here is my tummy, and here is my hat.
I'm a happy fellow, here's my nose,
I'm all snow from my head to my toes.

I have two bright eyes so I can see
All the snow falling down on me.
When the weather's cold, I'm strong and tall,
But when it's warm, I get very small.

Susan M. Paprocki
Northbrook, IL

Materials: White felt; needle and thread; felt scraps; glue; pair of scissors.

Making the Puppet: Use the pattern on page 70 as a guide to cut two hand puppet shapes out of white felt. Use the patterns on page 71 as guides to cut snow pal facial features, a hat shape, a scarf shape and several button shapes out of felt scraps and glue them to one of the hand puppet shapes. Put the two hand puppet shapes together and sew around the edges, leaving the bottom open.

Variations:

Groundhog Pop-Up Puppet

Groundhog, Groundhog

Groundhog, groundhog, popping up today.
Groundhog, groundhog, can you play?
If you see your shadow, hide away.
If there is no shadow, you can stay.
Groundhog, groundhog, popping up today.
Groundhog, groundhog, can you play?

Jean Warren

Materials: Styrofoam or paper cup; Styrofoam ball (small enough to fit inside the cup); straw; felt-tip markers; glue; pair of scissors.

Making the Puppet: Insert a straw into a Styrofoam ball. Pull the straw out, drop some glue into the hole, then replace the straw. Allow the glue to dry. Use felt-tip markers to draw groundhog ears, eyes, a nose and a mouth on the Styrofoam ball. Poke a hole in the bottom of a Styrofoam or paper cup. While holding the cup upright, stick the straw down into the cup and out the hole in the bottom.

Variations:

Queen of Hearts Paper Bag Puppet

Queen of Hearts
Sung to: "Three Blind Mice"

Queen of Hearts, Queen of Hearts,
Makes good tarts, makes good tarts.
She rolls and cuts and fills each pie
With jams and jellies, and that is why
We gobble them up and then we cry,
"More, more tarts! More, more tarts!"

Jean Warren

Materials: Small paper bag; construction paper; felt-tip markers; glue; pair of scissors.

Making the Puppet: Place a small paper bag flat on a table with the flap at the top. Use felt-tip markers to draw a face on the flap of the bag. Then decorate the puppet by gluing on a construction paper crown and various sizes of hearts as desired.

Variations:

Abe Lincoln Tongue Depressor Puppet

Abraham Lincoln
Sung to: "The Battle Hymn of the Republic"

Abraham Lincoln
Was the President, you know.
He led our land, America,
A long, long time ago.
He worked to put an end to war,
He worked to make men free.
That's why we all remember him, you see.

Vicki Claybrook
Kennewick, WA

Materials: Black felt; tongue depressor; felt-tip markers; glue.

Making the Puppet: Cut a top hat shape out of black felt and glue it to a tongue depressor. Use felt-tip markers to add a beard, other facial features and clothing shapes.

Variations:

Clothespin Pancake Man Puppet

Have You Seen the Pancake Man?
Sung to: "The Muffin Man"

Have you seen the Pancake Man,
The Pancake Man, the Pancake Man?
Have you seen the Pancake Man
Who jumped from the skillet and ran and ran?

He jumped from the skillet down to the floor,
To the floor, to the floor.
He jumped from the skillet down to the floor,
And ran and ran right out the door.

Jean Warren

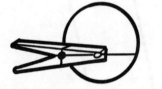

Materials: Small index card; spring-type clothespin; brown crayon; black felt-tip marker; glue; pair of scissors.

Making the Puppet: Cut a circle out of a small index card and color it with a brown crayon. Cut the circle in half, making the top half slightly larger than the bottom half. Glue the top half of the circle to the top side of a spring-type clothespin and the bottom half to the bottom side. Draw an eye on the top half with a black felt-tip marker. Squeeze the clothespin to make the puppet's mouth open and close.

Variations:

 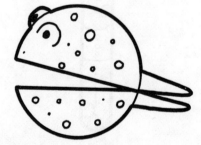 

Lion and Lamb Paper Plate Puppets

Like a Lion
Sung to: "Mary Had a Little Lamb"

March comes in like a lion,
Like a lion, like a lion.
March comes in like a lion,
And goes out like a lamb.

March comes in with a great big wind,
Great big wind, great big wind.
March comes in with a great big wind,
And goes out with a breeze.

June Meckel
Andover, MA

Materials: Paper plates; yellow yarn; cotton balls; felt-tip markers; tongue depressors; glue; pair of scissors.

Making the Puppets: To make the Lion Puppet, photocopy the lion face pattern on page 72. Color and cut out the face and glue it to the center of a paper plate. Cut yellow yarn into 2-inch pieces and glue them around the plate rim for a mane. To make the Lamb Puppet, photocopy the lamb face pattern on page 73. Color and cut out the face and glue it to the center of a paper plate. Fluff out cotton balls and glue them around the rim of the plate. Glue a tongue depressor handle to the back of each puppet.

Variations:

Leprechaun Styrofoam Ball Puppet

I'm a Little Leprechaun
Sung to: "I'm a Little Teapot"

I'm a little leprechaun, can you see?
I'm as tiny as I can be.
I come around just once a year,
When St. Patrick's Day is near.

Betty Ruth Baker
Waco, TX

Materials: Black and green felt; Styrofoam ball; pencil; cotton ball; felt scraps; glue; pair of scissors.

Making the Puppet: Cut two top hat shapes out of black felt. Glue the tops and sides of the shapes together. Then glue the hat to the top of a Styrofoam ball. Add small shamrock shapes cut out of green felt to the hat. Cut eye, nose and mouth shapes out of felt scraps and glue them to the Styrofoam ball. Fluff out a cotton ball and glue it below the mouth for a beard. Poke a hole in the bottom of the Styrofoam ball with a pencil. Remove the pencil and place the puppet on a finger.

Variations:

Caterpillar String Puppet

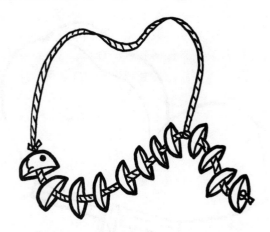

See the Caterpillar
Sung to: "Frere Jacques"

See the caterpillar, see the caterpillar,
Watch it crawl, watch it crawl.
See it crawling higher,
See it crawling higher,
Watch it crawl, up the wall.

See the caterpillar, see the caterpillar,
Watch it go, watch it go.
See it crawling lower,
See it crawling lower,
Way down low, to my toe.

See the caterpillar, see the caterpillar,
Watch it grin, watch it grin.
See it crawling higher,
See it crawling higher,
To my chin, to my chin.

Jean Warren

Materials: Egg carton; yarn; glue; pair of scissors.

Making the Puppet: Cut all of the egg cups out of an egg carton. Poke a hole in the bottom of each cup and string the cups on a piece of yarn to make a caterpillar. Tie knots in both ends of the yarn. Cut another piece of yarn and tie one end to the knot at the front of the caterpillar and the other end to the yarn near the eighth egg cup. Make the caterpillar crawl by holding onto the loop of yarn and moving it up and down.

Variation:

Butterfly Straw Puppet

Butterfly, Butterfly
Sung to: "Jingle Bells"

Butterfly, butterfly,
Dancing all around.
Butterfly, butterfly,
Now you're on the ground.
In a tree, hard to see,
Now you've flown away.
Butterfly, oh, butterfly,
Please come back some day.

Gee Gee Drysdale
Syracuse, NY

Materials: Construction paper or wallpaper; straw; pencil; crayons (if construction paper is used); stapler; pair of scissors.

Making the Puppet: Photocopy the butterfly pattern on page 74 and cut it out. Fold a piece of construction paper or wallpaper in half. Place the straight edge of the butterfly pattern on the fold, trace around it with a pencil and cut out the shape. Staple the shape along the fold as shown above. Then staple a straw onto the flap. If construction paper has been used, decorate the butterfly with crayons.

Variations:

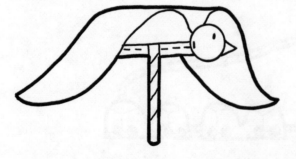 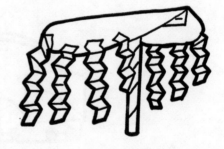

Willie Worm Surprise Puppet

Willie Worm

I have a pet named Willie,
Who lives at home with me.
I keep him in this special box,
So all my friends can see.

Where, oh, where is Willie?
Oh, where can Willie be?
Come out now, little Willie,
So all my friends can see.

He is a little timid.
I must be very firm.
Come out now, little Willie,
Come out, my Willie Worm.

Jean Warren

Materials: Small cardboard box; brown construction paper; construction paper scraps; brown felt-tip marker; glue; pair of scissors.

Making the Puppet: Cut a finger-sized hole in the bottom of a small cardboard box. Tear brown construction paper into tiny pieces and use them to fill the box half full. Color the outside of the box with a brown felt-tip marker and glue construction paper flowers around the top edges of the box. Hold the box upright in one hand and stick your index finger up through the hole, wiggling it like a worm.

Variations:

Pom-Pom Chick Puppets

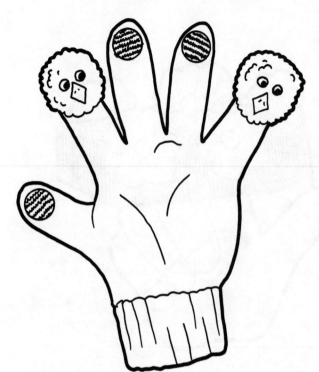

Down in the Barnyard
Sung to: "Down by the Station"

Down in the barnyard
Early in the morning,
See the little yellow chicks
Standing in a row.
See the busy farmer
Passing out their breakfast
Cheep, cheep, cheep, cheep,
Off they go.

Jean Warren

Materials: Glove; yellow pom-poms; Velcro fasteners; felt scraps; plastic moving eyes; glue; pair of scissors.

Making the Puppets: Glue one part of a two-part Velcro fastener to each finger of an old glove. Glue the second part of each Velcro fastener to a yellow pom-pom. Attach two plastic moving eyes to each pom-pom. Then glue on tiny beak shapes cut out of felt scraps. Use the velcro fasteners to attach the Pom-Pom Chicks to the glove.

Variations:

Walking Duck Puppet

I'm a Little Yellow Duck
Sung to: "Little White Duck"

I'm a little yellow duck
Who loves to see the rain.
A little yellow duck,
Now I will explain.
I love to see the rain come down,
So I can swim all around the town.
I'm a little yellow duck
Who loves to see the rain.
Splish, splish, splash!

Jean Warren

Materials: Yellow posterboard; felt-tip markers; pair of scissors.

Making the Puppet: Use the pattern on page 75 as a guide to cut a duck shape out of yellow posterboard. Cut two finger holes at the bottom of the puppet as indicated on the pattern. Use felt-tip markers to decorate the puppet as desired.

Variations:

Egg Carton Pig Puppet

This Little Piggy
Sung to: "Frere Jacques"

This little piggy, this little piggy,
Went to town, went to town.
He ran up and down,
He ran up and down,
Through the town, through the town.

This little piggy, this little piggy,
He stayed home, he stayed home.
He didn't like to roam,
He didn't like to roam,
He stayed home, he stayed home.

Jean Warren

Materials: Cardboard egg carton; pink tempera paint; paint brush; felt-tip markers; pair of scissors.

Making the Puppet: From a cardboard egg carton cut out, in one piece, an egg cup and two adjacent cones. Trim the cones to look like pig ears. Hold the egg cup so that the ears are on top and carefully cut an "x"-shape in the bottom side of the cup for a finger opening. Paint the puppet pink and add facial features with felt-tip markers.

Betty Silkunas
Lansdale, PA

Variations:

Buzzy Bee Balloon Puppet

Buzzy Bee
Sung to: "When Johnny Comes Marching Home"

Buzzy Bee is buzzing here
Around the room,
Buzzy Bee is buzzing there
Around the room.
Buzzy Bee flies to and fro,
Up on your head, down to your toe.
Oh, we're all so glad when
Buzzy Bee buzzes by.

Jean Warren

Materials: Yellow balloon; yellow ribbon; black permanent felt-tip marker.

Making the Puppet: Blow up a yellow balloon. Use a black permanent felt-tip marker to draw stripes around the balloon and two eyes close to the knot. Tie a loop of yellow ribbon around the knot.

Betty Silkunas
Lansdale, PA

Variations:

Little Dog Cup Puppet

Materials: Styrofoam or paper cup; construction paper; glue; pair of scissors.

Making the Puppet: Make a hole large enough for a finger on the side of a Styrofoam or paper cup. Lay the cup on its side with the hole on the bottom. Make a nose by cutting a large circle from construction paper and gluing it on what was the bottom of the cup. Glue two construction paper eyes on the sides of the cup. Then glue two construction paper ears to the rim.

Variations:

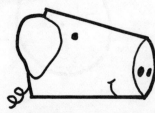

Frog Paper Plate Puppet

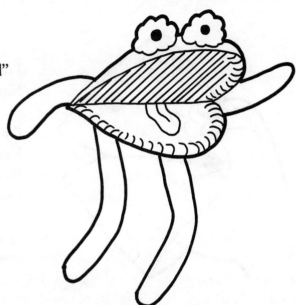

The Frog Lives in the Pond
Sung to: "The Farmer in the Dell"

The frog lives in the pond.
His tongue is oh, so long.
It reaches high to catch a fly.
The frog lives in the pond.

Jean Warren

Materials: Paper plate; cotton balls; green tempera paint; paint brush; green, black and red construction paper; glue; pair of scissors.

Making the Puppet: Fold a paper plate in half. Paint the outside of the plate green and let it dry. Cut two 1- by 6-inch strips out of construction paper. Glue one paper strip to the top half of the folded plate and the other strip to the bottom half to make hand holds. Glue two cotton balls on the rim of the top half of the plate for eyes. Attach a small circle of black construction paper to each cotton ball. Cut a long tongue shape out of red construction paper and glue it to the inside of the folded paper plate. Cut two 1- by 4-inch strips and two 1- by 6-inch strips out of green construction paper. Glue the shorter strips to the sides of the paper plate for arms and the longer strips to the bottom of the plate for legs.

Variations:

Fish Envelope Puppet

I'm a Fish
Sung to: "I'm a Little Teapot"

I'm a little fishy, I can swim.
Here is my tail, here is my fin.
When I want to have fun with my friends,
I wiggle my tail and dive right in.

Lynn Beaird
Loma Linda, CA

Materials: Business-sized envelope; felt-tip markers.

Making the Puppet: Tuck in the flap of a business-sized envelope. Place your hand inside the envelope with your fingers at one end and your thumb at the other. Indent the middle of the envelope toward your hand and fold your fingers and thumb together to make the puppet. Use felt-tip markers to draw on eyes, scales and fins. Open and close your hand to make the Fish Puppet talk and sing.

Variations:

Turtle Bowl Puppet

I'm a Little Green Turtle
Sung to: "Little White Duck"

I'm a little green turtle
My home is on my back.
A little green turtle,
Now what do you think of that?
I like to sit in the sun all day,
Catching bugs that fly my way.
I'm a little green turtle,
Who likes to eat all day.
Snap, snap, snap.

Jean Warren

Materials: Paper bowl; rubber band; green felt; green tempera paint; paint brush; glue; pair of scissors.

Making the Puppet: Paint the outside of a paper bowl with green tempera paint. Poke a small hole in the bottom. Insert a length of rubber band through the hole and knot the end on the inside of the bowl. Use the pattern on page 76 as a guide to cut a turtle body shape out of green felt. Glue the rim of the bowl to the top of the felt shape so that the legs, head and tail are showing.

Variations:

Alligator Egg Carton Puppet

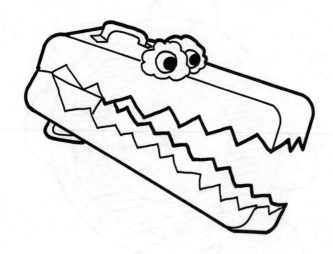

Mr. Alligator
Sung to: "Frere Jacques"

Mr. Alligator, Mr. Alligator,
Don't you bite, don't you bite!
I can run away from you,
I can run away from you,
Out of sight, out of sight.

Claudia G. Reid

Materials: Egg cartons; plastic moving eyes; cotton balls; construction paper; tape; glue; pair of scissors.

Making the Puppet: Cut the lids off two egg cartons. Cut jagged teeth around three edges of each lid, leaving one short edge uncut. Put the lids together, with the teeth facing inward, and tape the uncut ends together. Cut two 1- by 6-inch strips out of construction paper and tape one near the back of the top lid and the other near the back of the bottom lid to make hand holds. Glue two cotton balls on the top lid and attach a plastic moving eye to each one.

Variations:

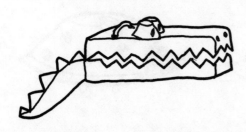  

Dinosaur Sock Puppet

Dinosaurs
Sung to: "Oh, My Darling Clementine"

Great big dinosaurs, great big dinosaurs,
Lived so very long ago.
Some liked land and some liked water,
Some flew in the air.

Great big dinosaurs, great big dinosaurs,
Lived so very long ago.
Some had horns and some had spikes,
Some had wings like bats.

Great big dinosaurs, great big dinosaurs,
Lived so very long ago.
Some ate plants and some ate meat,
But now there are no more.

Allane Eastberg, Jennifer Eastberg
Gig Harbor, WA

Materials: Athletic tube sock; needle and thread; felt; pair of scissors.

Making the Puppet: Cut a 2- by 8-inch strip out of felt. Make diagonal cuts along one of the long sides of the felt strip. Sew the uncut edge of the felt strip to an athletic tube sock, starting about 2 inches from the toe. Then sew a small felt triangle on each side of the felt strip for eyes. Put your hand in the sock and pull the toe in slightly. Sew another felt triangle where the sock folds in to make a tongue.

Variations:

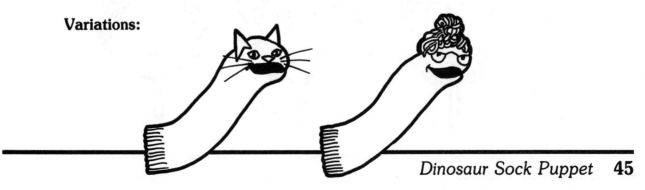

Sun Circle Puppet

Bright Sun
Sung to: "Row, Row, Row Your Boat"

Bright sun shining down,
Shining on the ground.
What a lovely face you have,
Yellow, big and round.

Susan A. Miller
Kutztown, PA

Materials: Yellow self-stick paper; yellow yarn; felt-tip markers; Popsicle stick; pair of scissors.

Making the Puppet: Cut two 4-inch circles out of yellow self-stick paper. Remove the backing from one of the circles. Cut yellow yarn into short pieces and place them around the edges of the sticky side of the circle to make sun rays. Remove the backing from the second circle and place it on top of the first circle, sticky sides together, with a Popsicle stick handle in between. Use felt-tip markers to add facial features.

Kay Roozen
Des Moines, IA

Variations:

Hula Dancer Whisk Broom Puppet

Swing and Sway
Sung to: "Frere Jacques"

Swing and sway, swing and sway,
Move this way, move this way.
Let's all do the hula,
Let's all do the hula.
Swing and sway, move this way.

Jean Warren

Materials: Whisk broom; felt scraps; glue; pair of scissors.

Making the Puppet: Hold the handle of a whisk broom so that the bristles are pointing down. Cut a mouth shape and two eye shapes out of felt scraps and glue them near the top of the broom. Then cut small flower shapes out of different colors of felt and glue them just below the puppet's face to form a lei.

Variations:

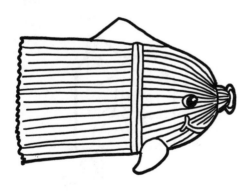 

Robot Box Puppet

Robot Song
Sung to: "Did You Ever See a Lassie?"

Did you ever see a robot,
A robot, a robot?
Did you ever see a robot
March down the street?
He teeters and totters,
And teeters and totters.
Did you ever see a robot
March down the street?

Jean Warren

Materials: Empty detergent box, cracker box or cereal box; cardboard toilet tissue tubes; aluminum foil; construction paper; glue; pair of scissors.

Making the Puppet: Cut the lid off an empty detergent box, cracker box or cereal box and turn it upside down. Cut holes in the narrow sides of the box and insert cardboard toilet tissue tubes for arms. Cover the box and the toilet tissue tubes with aluminum foil. Cut facial features out of construction paper and glue them to the front of the box. Put your hand inside the box to work the puppet.

Variations:

Popsicle Stick Car Puppet

My Car
Sung to: "She'll Be Coming Round the Mountain"

I'll be driving a red Ford when I come.
I'll be driving a red Ford when I come.
I'll be driving a red Ford,
I'll be driving a red Ford,
I'll be driving a red Ford when I come.

Substitute the name of the color and make of
any car for the words "red Ford."

Jean Warren

Materials: Magazine; posterboard; Popsicle stick; glue; pair of scissors.

Making the Puppet: Cut out a magazine picture of a car. Glue the picture to a piece of posterboard and trim around the edges. Then glue a Popsicle stick handle to the back of the posterboard.

Variations:

Nosy Rosie Cup Puppet

Nosy Rosie
Sung to: "The Mulberry Bush"

Here comes old Nosy Rosie,
Nosy Rosie, Nosy Rosie.
Here comes old Nosy Rosie,
Sniff, sniff, sniffing flowers.

Repeat, substituting for "flowers" the names of
other things that Nosy Rosie can sniff.

Jean Warren

Materials: Styrofoam or paper cup; felt-tip markers; yarn; glue; pair of scissors.

Making the Puppet: Cut a small circle out of the side of a Styrofoam or paper cup to make a nose hole. Add eyes and a mouth with felt-tip markers. Glue pieces of yarn on top of the cup for hair. Stick a finger into the cup and out the hole to make Rosie's nose. If you wish to hide your hand, stick your finger up through the middle of a paper napkin before poking it through the paper cup.

Variations:

Bertha Bottle Puppet

Bertha Bottle
Sung to: "Old MacDonald Had a Farm"

Bertha Bottle is my friend,
She is lots of fun.
She can jump and turn around,
I can make her run.
She can jump up here,
She can jump up there,
Here a jump, there a jump,
Everywhere a jump, jump.
Bertha Bottle is my friend,
She is lots of fun.

Claudia G. Reid

Materials: Empty dishwashing liquid bottle; fabric; felt-tip markers; yarn; glue; pair of scissors.

Making the Puppet: Rinse and dry an empty dishwashing liquid bottle and discard the cap. Hold the bottle upside down. Glue a piece of fabric around the bottle, leaving one-third of the bottle uncovered for a face. Use felt-tip markers to draw two eyes, a nose and a mouth on the face part of the bottle and glue pieces of yarn to the top of the bottle for hair.

Variations:

Lemon and Lime Rhythm Puppets

The Lemon and Lime Shake
Sung to: "The Hokey-Pokey"

You put the lemon shaker in,
You put the lemon shaker out.
You put the lemon shaker in,
And you shake it all about.
You do the lemon shake
And you turn yourself around.
That's what it's all about.

You put the lime shaker in,
You put the lime shaker out.
You put the lime shaker in,
And you shake it all about.
You do the lime shake
And you turn yourself around.
That's what it's all about.

Jean Warren

Materials: Plastic lemon- and lime-shaped containers; unsharpened pencils; felt scraps; yarn; glue; pair of scissors.

Making the Puppets: Remove the lids from a plastic lemon-shaped container and a plastic lime-shaped container. Stick an unsharpened pencil through each opening to make a handle. Cut eye, nose, mouth and ear shapes out of felt scraps. Glue the shapes on the containers. Add yarn pieces for hair.

Variations:

Dish Mop Puppet

Little Dish Mop
Sung to: "Little White Duck"

I'm a little dish mop
Who likes to work and work.
A little dish mop
Who scrubs out all the dirt.
I like to scrub and scrub all day,
Then rinse off so I can play.
I'm a little dish mop
Who likes to work and work.
Scrub, scrub, scrub!

Jean Warren

Materials: Dish mop; felt scraps; plastic moving eyes; glue; pair of scissors.

Making the Puppet: Hold the dish mop so that the mop is at the top. Part the strings down the middle and flatten them. Make a puppet face on this flat area by gluing on plastic moving eyes and other facial features cut out of felt scraps.

Variations:

Hairbrush Puppet

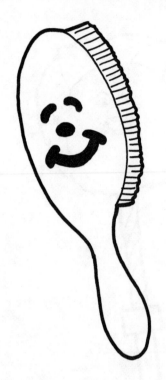

Brush Your Hair
Sung to: "Jingle Bells"

Brush your hair, brush your hair,
Give your hair a treat.
Part it, braid it, brush it back,
But always keep it neat.
Brush it once, brush it twice,
Keep it nice and clean.
Always brush the tangles out
And see the lovely sheen!

Lynn Beaird
Loma Linda, CA

Materials: Hairbrush; felt scraps; glue; pair of scissors.

Making the Puppet: Cut two eye shapes, a nose shape and a mouth shape out of felt scraps. Glue the shapes to the back of a hairbrush.

Variations:

MacBurger Puppet

Old MacBurger
Sung to: "Old MacDonald Had a Farm"

Old MacBurger had a mouth,
E-I-E-I-O.
And in this mouth he put some food,
E-I-E-I-O.
With a munch, munch here,
And a munch, munch there,
Here a munch, there a munch,
Everywhere a munch, munch.
Old MacBurger had a mouth,
E-I-E-I-O.

Jean Warren

Materials: Styrofoam or cardboard hamburger holder; plastic moving eyes; black felt-tip marker; glue; pair of scissors.

Making the Puppet: Cut the fastener tabs off a Styrofoam or cardboard hamburger holder. Glue two plastic moving eyes on the front of the holder and add a mouth with a black felt-tip marker. Carefully poke a hole in the back of the lid and another hole near the back in the bottom of the holder. To use the puppet, put your index finger through the hole in the lid and your thumb through the hole in the bottom. Then move your finger and thumb up and down.

Variations:

French Fry Holder Marching Band Puppet

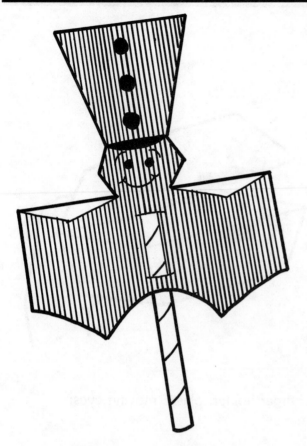

Number March Sung to:
"Skip to My Lou"

Marching together, one by one,
Marching together, one by one,
Marching together, one by one.
Marching together, oh, what fun!

Additional verses: "Marching together two by two;
three by three; four by four;" etc.

Betty Ruth Baker
Waco, TX

Materials: Cardboard French fry holder; straw; felt-tip markers; pair of scissors.

Making the Puppet: Carefully open up a cardboard French fry holder and use felt-tip markers to draw a face in the middle of the inside. Add other details as desired. Fold back the sides of the holder to make shoulders. Cut two horizontal slits in the holder. Then weave a straw through the slits to make a handle.

Variations:

Millie Milk Carton Puppet

Millie Milk Carton
Sung to: "Frere Jacques"

Millie Milk Carton, Millie Milk Carton,
Time to eat, time to eat.
Open up your mouth,
Open up your mouth.
Here's a treat, here's a treat.

Let the children take turns placing dried beans or
macaroni into Millie's mouth as they sing the song.

Claudia G. Reid

Materials: Empty half-gallon cardboard milk carton; construction paper;
felt-tip markers; yarn; tape; craft knife; pair of scissors.

Making the Puppet: Thoroughly wash and dry an empty half-gallon cardboard milk carton. On the back of the carton, poke a hole through the
top. Insert a piece of yarn through the hole and knot the end on the inside
of the carton. Then tape the top closed and cover the entire carton with
construction paper, letting the yarn hang free. Approximately one-third of
the way down, cut through three sides of the carton with a craft knife. Use
felt-tip markers to draw eyes and a nose on the top half of the carton and
a mouth around the cut. Add pieces of yarn for hair.

Variations:

Dancing Spoon Puppet

Have You Seen My Dancing Puppet?
Sung to: "The Muffin Man"

Have you seen my dancing puppet,
My dancing puppet, my dancing puppet?
Have you seen my dancing puppet
Twirl round and round and round?

Jean Warren

Materials: Wooden spoon; fabric; felt-tip markers; yarn; tape; glue; pair of scissors.

Making the Puppet: Use felt-tip markers to draw a face on one side of a wooden spoon. Cut a circle out of fabric and make a slit in the middle. Stick the handle of the spoon through the slit. Hold the head of the puppet upside down and tape the fabric around the neck. Turn the puppet upright so that the fabric drapes over the spoon handle like a smock. Glue on pieces of yarn for hair.

Variations:

Goldilocks Folded Paper Finger Puppet

Goldilocks
Sung to: "Yankee Doodle"

Once a girl named Goldilocks
Went to see three bears.
She tasted all their porridge,
Then sat in all their chairs.
Looking for a place to sleep,
Which bed would she choose?
She hopped into the baby bear's bed
And took a little snooze.

Jean Warren

Materials: Construction paper; paper clip; felt-tip markers; yellow yarn; pair of scissors.

Making the Puppet: Cut a 5- by 7-inch rectangle out of construction paper. Fold the rectangle in half lengthwise and then in half again to make a long narrow strip. Curl one of the short ends down halfway and paper clip it to the middle of the strip. Use felt-tip markers to draw a face on the loop. Then tie several pieces of yellow yarn over the top of the loop for hair.

Variations:

Fingertip Friend Puppets

Friends Are Special
Sung to: "Frere Jacques"

Friends are special, friends are special,
Make a few, make a few.
Smile and say "How are you?"
Smile and say "How are you?
I like you, I like you!"

Karen Leslie
Erie, PA

Materials: Glove; felt-tip markers; yarn; glue; pair of scissors.

Making the Puppets: Cut the fingertips off an old glove. Use felt-tip markers to add facial features to the fingertips. Glue pieces of yarn on the tops of the fingertips for hair. Put one puppet on each finger of one hand.

Sarah Cooper
Ft. Worth, TX

Variations:

Finger Face Family Puppets

Family Picnic
Sung to: "The Teddy Bears' Picnic"

Let's all go to the woods today,
We're sure of a big surprise.
Let's all go to the woods today,
We'll walk there side by side.
We know that we'll have lots of fun,
We'll eat and play and dance and run.
Today's the day we have our family picnic!

Jean Warren

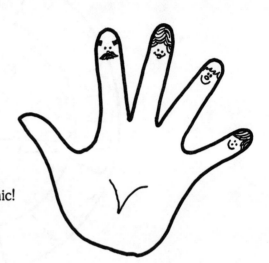

Materials: Felt-tip markers.

Making the Puppets: Use felt-tip markers to draw two eyes, a nose and a mouth on each finger of one hand. Use your Finger Face Puppets in the Finger Puppet Theater. (Directions for making the theater are on page 62.)

Variations:

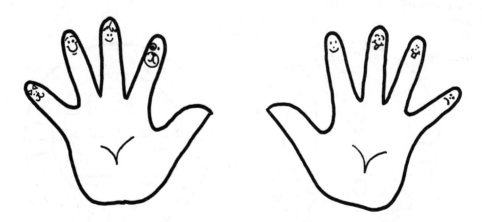

Paper Plate Finger Puppet Theater

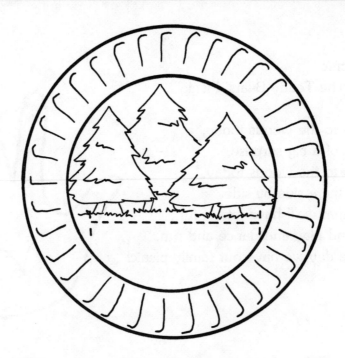

Materials: Paper plate; crayons; tape; pair of scissors.

Making the Theater: Photocopy the pattern on page 77. Color the pattern and cut it out. Glue the pattern to the middle of a paper plate. Cut a horizontal slit in the center of the paper plate, as indicated by the dotted line on the pattern. Cover each side of the slit with tape to prevent paper cuts. Make a 1-inch vertical cut at each end of the slit.

Barbara Robinson
Glendale, AZ

Variations:

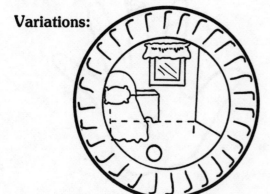 

Puppet Patterns

Nursery Rhyme Puppet Pattern

Nursery Rhyme Puppet Pattern **65**

Circus Shadow Puppet Pattern **67**

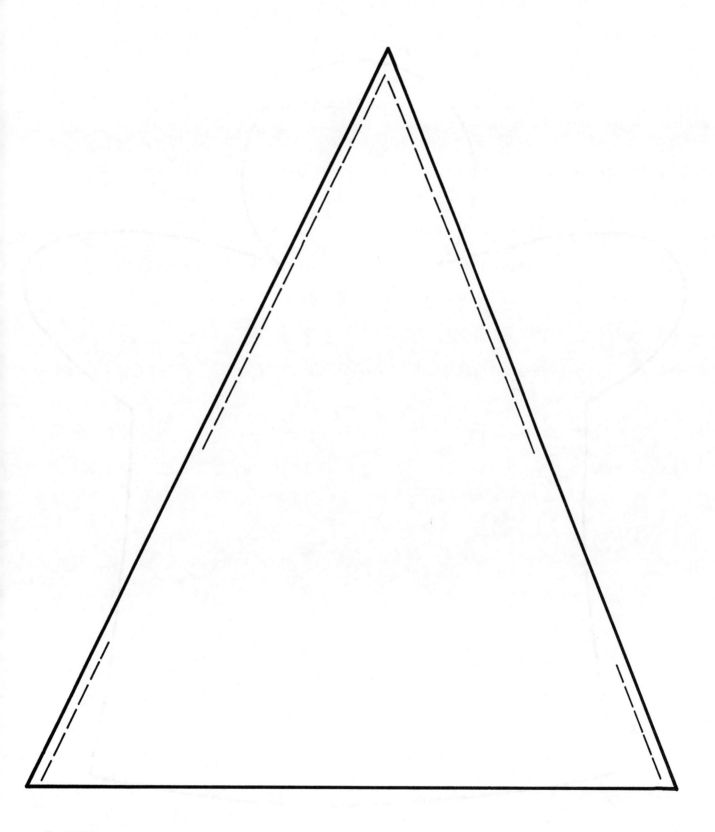

Santa Felt Triangle Puppet Pattern **69**

70 *Snow Pal Felt Hand Puppet Pattern*

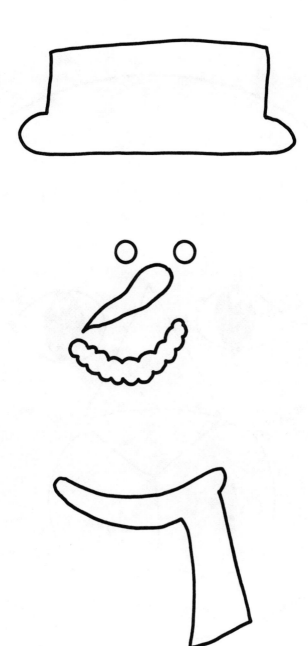

Snow Pal Felt Hand Puppet Pattern **71**

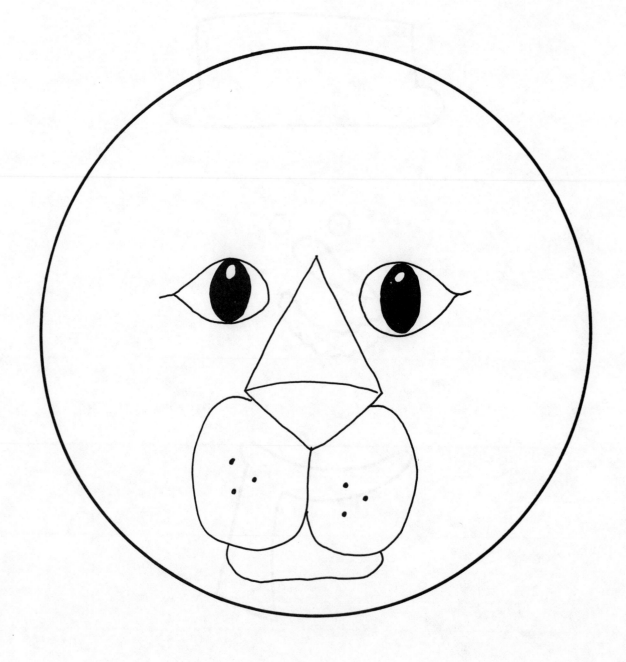

Lamb Paper Plate Puppet **73**

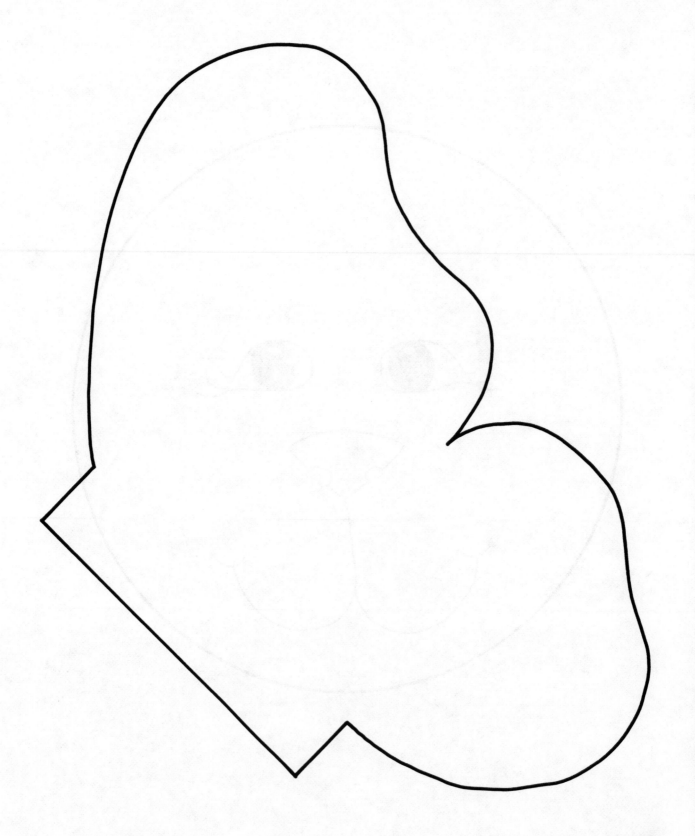

74 *Butterfly Straw Puppet Pattern*

Walking Duck Puppet Pattern　**75**

Turtle Bowl Puppet Pattern

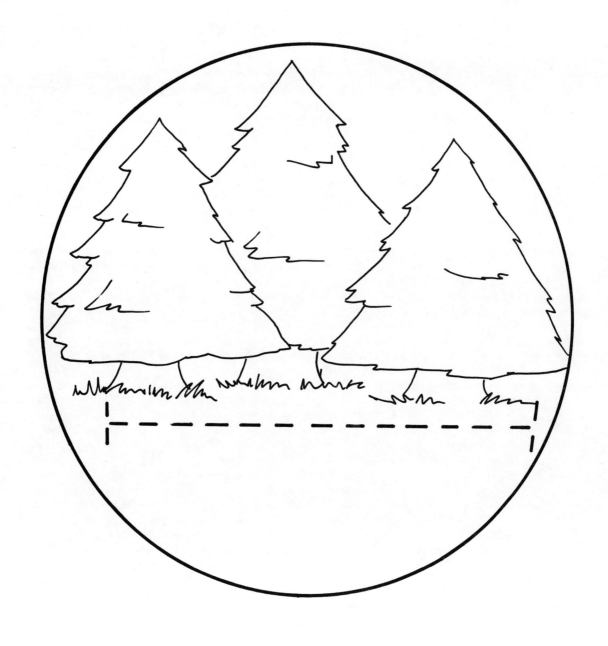

Paper Plate Finger Puppet Theater Pattern **77**

Activities, songs and new ideas to use right now are waiting for you in every issue of the TOTLINE newsletter.

Each issue puts the fun into teaching with 24 pages of challenging and creative activities for young children, including open-ended art activities, learning games, music, language and science activities.

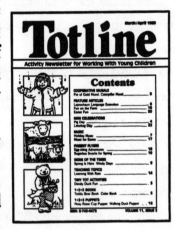

Sample issue $1.00

One year subscription (6 issues) $15.00

Beautiful bulletin boards, games and flannelboards are easy with PRESCHOOL PATTERNS.

You won't want to miss a single issue of PRESCHOOL PATTERNS with 3 large sheets of patterns delightfully and simply drawn. Each issue includes patterns for making flannelboard characters, bulletin boards, learning games and more!

Sample issue $2.00

One year subscription (6 issues) $18.00

ORDER FROM:
Warren Publishing House, Inc. • P.O. Box 2250, Dept. B • Everett, WA 98203

Totline Books

Super Snacks – 120 seasonal sugarless snack recipes kids love.

Teaching Tips – 300 helpful hints for working with young children.

Teaching Toys – over 100 toy and game ideas for teaching learning concepts.

Piggyback Songs – 110 original songs, sung to the tunes of childhood favorites.

More Piggyback Songs – 195 more original songs.

Piggyback Songs for Infants and Toddlers – 160 original songs, for infants and toddlers.

Piggyback Songs in Praise of God – 185 original religious songs, sung to familiar tunes.

Piggyback Songs in Praise of Jesus – 240 more original religious songs.

Holiday Piggyback Songs – over 240 original holiday songs.

1•2•3 Art – over 200 open-ended art activities.

1•2•3 Games – 70 no-lose games for ages 2 to 8.

1•2•3 Colors – over 500 Color Day activities for young children.

1•2•3 Puppets – over 50 puppets to make for working with young children.

1•2•3 Murals – over 50 murals to make with children's open-ended art.

1•2•3 Books – over 20 beginning books to make for working with young children.

Teeny-Tiny Folktales – 15 folktales from around the world plus flannelboard patterns.

Short-Short Stories – 18 original stories plus seasonal activities.

Mini-Mini Musicals – 10 simple musicals, sung to familiar tunes.

Small World Celebrations – 16 holidays from around the world to celebrate with young children.

"Cut & Tell" Scissor Stories for Fall – 8 original stories plus patterns.

"Cut & Tell" Scissor Stories for Winter – 8 original stories plus patterns.

"Cut & Tell" Scissor Stories for Spring – 8 original stories plus patterns.

Seasonal Fun – 50 two-sided reproducible parent flyers.

Theme-A-Saurus – the great big book of mini teaching themes.

Available at school supply stores and parent/teacher stores or write for our FREE catalog.

Warren Publishing House, Inc. • P.O. Box 2250, Dept. B • Everett, WA 98203